Curiosity
Projects

CONTENTS

Dedicated to Dr. Marsha Grace, bonfire of hopeful curiosity, and Beth Hoeppner for her indignant insistence that Curiosity Projects were a flame worth fanning.

Special thanks to Mike Jackson, Sammi Smith, and Claire Grady for co-conspiring and co-developing Curiosity Projects over the years.

A Bill of Rights for Curious Learning

By Scot Hoffman, Suzie Boss, and Barry Dyck

The right to:

- Choose my learning topic or pursuit
- Learn about something that inspires or delights me
- Ask questions that matter to me
- Play to learn
- Learn to play
- Make stuff
- Create my learning path
- Make mistakes and "fail" while learning
- Change my learning path
- Pursue help from an expert
- Become an expert at any age
- Learn about the same topic again and again and again
- Learn about something others don't value
- Share what I've learned with others
- Learn from other curious learners
- Be inspired by curious learners
- Inspire others with my curiosity
- Satisfy my curiosity

Introduction

This is a book about a flexible, adaptable practice called Curiosity Projects, that can help school systems, classroom teachers, and parents personalize learning by providing time, structure, choice, and coaching that enables students to use their curiosity to start and drive their learning.

What Are Curiosity Projects?

Curiosity Projects are adaptable, structured units of study that support schools, teachers, and parents to help students learn how to learn by using their curiosity (the gap between what they know and what they want or need to know) and emulating how curious learners learn. Curiosity Projects enable students to focus on exploring these key questions as they learn:

- What is curiosity?
- What does curiosity look like?
- What do curious learners do to start their learning?
- How do curious learners gather information?
- How do curious learners share their information?

Curiosity Projects are **adaptable** units that teachers or parents create to *structure* learning where students:

- Learn how curious learners use their curiosity
- Self-determine a learning topic or pursuit
- Use *their* curiosity to make decisions about their learning
- Are provided adequate time, support, and resources to pursue in-depth learning
- Have an opportunity to share with peers, family, friends, or other meaningful audiences.

Curiosity and Learning

According to Piotrowski, Litman, & Valkenburg (2014), there are two different kinds of curiosity that fuel our desire to explore, gain experience, and acquire knowledge. The first type, called I-Type Curiosity, is related to positive feelings of interest associated with anticipating learning something new. The second type of curiosity, D-Type Curiosity, is related to unpleasant experiences of uncertainty and feeling deprived of information. When people experience I-Type Curiosity, they are compelled by the intrinsic enjoyment of new discoveries. When people experience D-Type Curiosity, they are compelled by the discomfort or frustration of an incomplete understanding or the need to solve a specific problem (Piotrowski, Litman, & Valkenburg, 2014).

Behavioral economist George Loewenstein describes Curiosity as a gap in our knowledge. No matter, how you define it, it seems that Curiosity can be a powerful force that compels us to learn. Experiencing or learning something new - satisfying one's curiosity, might reduce curiosity, but Lowenstein says that as we gain more information, we are more likely to be increasingly aware and curious about what we do not know (Heath & Heath, 2007).

In addition to the research on what Curiosity is and how it fuels our desire for learning, two new studies using functional magnetic resonance imaging (fMRI) show that when we are curious about something, finding the answers to those questions activates areas of the brain associated with rewards. The result is significantly enhanced memory of new information that fills the curiosity gap created by the questions that make us curious. Additionally, having a question we are curious about and anticipating the answer also seems to activate our brains, increasing our ability to remember other surrounding or incidental information (Gruber, Gelman, & Ranganath, 2014, Kang et al., 2009). Gruber et al speculate that the large and lasting effects of curiosity on memory for interesting information in their study are likely to underestimate the impact of curiosity on learning in daily life.

While evidence of curiosity as a driver for learning and its effect on remembering what we learn, curiosity appears to be lacking in our schools.

Researcher Susan Engel has investigated the prevalance of curiosity in elementary school classrooms. While observing in kindergarten classrooms she found that, while activity was educationally productive, students were not coming up with questions. In each two hour block of observation, Kindergarten students asked from 2 to 5 questions about something they wanted to know about or learn. In fifth grade these curiosity questions were more sparse. In a typical 2 hour block of time, 5th grade students weren't asking about anything they wanted to know (Engel, 2013).

Engel (2013) hypothesized that adult influence may be a major factor. In her investigations, busy teachers tended to avoid the few curious questions that students asked in order to move forward with learning activities and lessons. She further notes that student curiosity and curious questions increase when an adult visibly models or shares his or her curiosity for learning. In summarizing her findings, Engel states, "For children to develop and satisfy their urge to know, they need role models, opportunities to practice, and guidance" (p. 36).

In order for curiosity to flourish as a personal drive for learning, schools and parents must intentionally model how curiosity drives learning, and intentionally create the time, structures, choices and coaching that helps learners to use their curiosity to power and enhance their learning.

Why Curiosity Projects are Important

There are three reasons that schools, teachers, and parents need Curiosity Projects. The first is that increasing numbers of our students today are uninspired and disengaged. The second reason is that students who are living in a long-tail world, where learning is already pervasively personalized, require truly personalized learning options. The third reason is that research is beginning to show that curiosity plays a role in remembering what we learn.

Uninspired Learning

According to Thrash & Elliot (2004), Inspiration has three core characteristics. First, inspiration points or pulls us towards something that is better or more important than our usual concerns. Second, inspiration is something evoked in us, that moves or strikes us. We don't choose to be inspired. Inspiration, in effect, chooses us. The third characteristic of inspiration is motivation. We feel compelled to do *something* with whatever it is that inspires us. Schools that don't create time and space and coaching for students to act on and learn about what inspires them are uninspiring (Thrash & Elliot, 2004).

Think back on your own formal schooling. Think of the times when your interest, intense curiosity, or pangs of inspiration were the school-sponsored rationale and drivers of your learning. You can probably think about many instances when what you were learning resulted in interest, intense curiosity, or pangs of inspiration. But can you think of a class, or a course where your interest, curiosity, or inspiration were the school/teacher-sponsored starting point, spark and rationale for *your* learning? Or think about your children and your students. How often do their interests, intense curiosities, pangs of inspiration, or passions get to be the starting point for their learning?

The current world of schooling that our students exist in is too slow, too small, too convergent, and too close-ended to support inspired learning for our students. Dewey's nearly 100 year old description of students pretending to be engaged in school while their hearts and minds are otherwise engaged, is pervasively true in schools. A 2014 Gallup poll of US schools shows that 53% of 5th-12th grade students report being engaged in school while the other 47% report being disengaged or actively disengaged in school (Gallup Student Poll, 2014). In the US, this problem translates into a societal problem where roughly one-third of workers report being engaged in their work and the other two-thirds report being disengaged, or actively disengaged in their work (Adkins, 2015).

In his essay, *The Importance of Falling in Love with Something*, Paul Torrance, the creator of the Torrance Test of Creative Thinking, reflects on a 22 year longitudinal study focused on the connection between the third, fourth, and fifth graders and their passions and projections of their future careers. In the essay, he explores the differences between students who grew up to *play the games of themselves* and students who grew up to *play the games of others.* From this study he had this to say about the importance of people (students) playing the games of themselves:

"I am convinced that the driving force behind future accomplishments is the image of the future of people. Positive images of the future are a powerful and magnetic force. These images of the future draw us on and energize us. Giving us the courage and will to take important initiatives and move forward to new solutions and achievements. To dream and to plan, to be curious about the future and to wonder how much it can be influenced by our efforts are important aspects of our being human" (Torrance, 1983, p. 72). He goes even further, noting that "History also warns that societies that lack vigorous, realistic images of the future perish."

Learning in the Long Tail
"Up until now, the focus has been on dozens of markets of millions, instead of millions of markets of dozens." (Joe Kraus, CEO of Jot-Spot)

"The theory of the Long Tail is that our culture and economy is increasingly shifting away from a focus on a relatively small number of 'hits' (mainstream products and markets) at the head of the demand curve and toward a huge number of niches in the tail. As the costs of production and distribution fall, especially online, there is now less need to lump products and consumers [and students] into one-size-fits-all containers" (Anderson, 2015).

The theory of the long tail doesn't just apply to business models and companies like Amazon, Netflix, and Google who outperform other companies by meeting the needs and interests of millions of people outside of the mainstream markets. The theory of the long tail increasingly describes the everyday world that we and our students live in.

I have seen the long tail world of my six-year old daughter this week as she watched her favorite show, *Tiny House Nation* on FYI network. The show is about building and living in houses that are smaller than her bedroom. Until recently, I didn't know that there was a tiny house movement, or that FYI was a television network. Or, that a six year-old could be obsessed with the construction of tiny houses. Her other favorite show? It's *How to Make Your Own Homemade Paper (http://bit.ly/paperalice)*. Actually, this is a YouTube Video with an uncapitalized title by someone who calls herself Paper Alice. Paper Alice also has a nation, made up of viewers wanting to learn how to make their own recycled paper. The long tail world we are living in is getting longer every day. There are more channels, more books, more products, more choices, and more information on the way. Will my daughter grow up to become one of the dozens of millions: a teacher, nurse, engineer, carpenter, chef, or something easily recognizable and describable? Or, will she become something that isn't a thing yet? It seems just as likely she will become one of the millions of dozens. Maybe she'll have her own nation.

The upshot is that the long tail world has Personalized Learning already. Schools are struggling to catch up and stay relevant in a world where students can learn anything, anywhere, anytime. Learning must move from a myopic focus on the dozens of learning topics for the millions and grow their capacity to support Personalized Learning where there are millions of topics that enable and empower students to grow their capacity to learn what they need, when they need it. Being a curious learner who knows how to use their curiosity to learn what they want or need to know, is not a narcissistic extension of an everybody-gets-a-trophy world. In the long tail world, Personalized Learning is the new essential way to learn and navigate our world.

tagxedo.com

Skilled Personalized Learning is not just something for the distant future. It's essential now! In his HBR article *21st-Century Talent Spotting: Why Potential Now Trumps Brains, Experience, and "Competencies"*, HR expert Claudio Fernández-Aráoz makes the case that in a rapidly accelerating change environment, the ability to learn how to learn trumps just about everything. He describes these as the hallmarks of potential:

"Curiosity: a penchant for seeking out new experiences, knowledge, and candid feedback and an openness to learning and change.

Insight: the ability to gather and make sense of information that suggests new possibilities.

Engagement: a knack for using emotion and logic to communicate a persuasive vision and connect with people.

Determination: the wherewithal to fight for difficult goals despite challenges and to bounce back from adversity." (Fernández-Aráoz, 2014, p. 8)

Intrinsic Motivation

"To be self-determined is to endorse one's actions at the highest level of reflection. When self-determined, people experience a sense of freedom to do what is interesting, personally important, and self vitalizing." - Edward Deci & Richard Ryan

Conditions that Foster Intrinsic Motivation

Curiosity Projects are based on intentionally using curiosity to learn and by providing the psychological needs we all have for Autonomy, Competence, and Relatedness to Others. These psychological needs have been intentionally leveraged by organizations such as 3M and Google, and by Apple, LinkedIn, and other companies in order to optimize intrinsic motivation to drive productivity and innovation. In corporate settings, these practices work by giving employees time and freedom to work towards developing new products of their choosing. These practices have resulted in innovations such as Post-It notes, Gmail, and many others.

Meeting these needs has been shown to result in increased intrinsic motivation for learning. Students whose needs for Autonomy, Competence, and Relatedness to Others is supported in the classroom, experience positive academic, cognitive, and affective outcomes (Reeve, 2002; Guay, Ratelle, & Chanal, 2008). In other words, students who are autonomously motivated perform better at school, learn concepts more deeply, and enjoy school. They also demonstrate greater motivation to master what they learn, greater perceived competence, intrinsic motivation, and positive emotions about school (Reeve, Jang, Carrell, Jeon & Barch, 2004). The research is clear about the positive impacts of intrinsic motivation for learning in school that supports many of our own adult experiences - if we are intrinsically motivated, we engage deeply and develop passion for our learning and our work (Hoffman, 2014, p. 10).

The need for Autonomy, the need for Competence, and the need for Relatedness to Others are the three conditions that foster intrinsic motivation for learning. Of these, the need for Autonomy is the most important need that must be met. These conditions support intrinsic motivation during Curiosity Projects:

Condition of Autonomy - Learners have control over their learning. Learners choose the topic or subject they are curious about or interested in, and they make the important learning decisions throughout the course of learning. Loss of control of Curiosity Projects thwart the intrinsic motivation they were created to foster.

Condition of Competence - Learners have the feeling of gaining knowledge, skill, and mastery. Learners use their curiosity to generate questions or design experiences that result in new knowledge and skills.

Condition of Relatedness to Others - Learners experience connection to peers or other important people during the Curiosity Projects.

Curiosity Projects require that students:

- Self-determine a learning topic or pursuit (**condition of Autonomy**)
- Are provided adequate time, support, and resources to pursue in-depth learning (**condition of Competence**)
- Have an opportunity to share with peers, family, friends, or other meaningful audiences (**condition of Relatedness to Others**).

A Structure that Creates the Conditions for Intrinsic Motivation

One of the main misconceptions about giving students control over the topics, questions, and pathways for their learning is that student autonomy is synonymous with a lack of structure. Providing students with a high degree of autonomy requires thoughtful structuring and coaching.

Don Holdaway, a pioneer of modern literacy, created the Big Book, the practice of Shared Reading, and the Natural Learning Model which is the basis of the literacy instructional practices of Reader's Workshop and Writer's Workshop. The Natural Learning Model consists of:

Demonstration - Learners are immersed in purposeful environments. Skilled practitioners share and demonstrate skills or strategies in a meaningful context and invite learners to try to use those skills or strategies.

Participation - Learners choose which skills and strategies they want to try. Teachers, parents, or coaches identify and respond to learner's efforts to use new skills and strategies.

Practice - Learners engage in independent practice and self-correction employing skills and strategies with teaching or coaching support close at hand.

Performance - Learners are invited to share and become the demonstrators, using skills and strategies for purposeful means, to an authentic audience. (Weaver, 2002)

Curiosity Projects in classrooms are typically structured around a daily mini lesson where teachers or curious experts **demonstrate** a useful skill or strategy that curious learners use (about 10 minutes). Next, students have Individual work time where they engage in **independent practice** by choosing from a menu of clearly understood learning options such as: developing questions, using a variety of texts to find information about their topics, composing interview questions, or planning to share what they have learned. During this time, students have access to tools, resources, and **teacher support** by conferring with individual students or small groups of students. When Curiosity Projects are completed, learners participate in some form of **performance** where they become demonstrators, sharing their knowledge, skills, and strategies for learning with peers, and possibly other audiences they value.

Uncovering What Curious Learners Do

In the case of Curiosity Projects, teaching and demonstration focus on uncovering how curious learners use their curiosity by inquiring into these broad questions:

- How do curious learners use their curiosity to initiate their learning?
- How do curious learners gather information?
- How do curious learners share information?
- How do curious learners reflect on their learning?

Template for Curiosity Projects

This chapter is a detailed template for Curiosity Projects. This template was originally used as a guide for Curiosity Projects as a homework project for Elementary School students over the course of six weeks. It is written for parents of second grade students. However, Curiosity Projects, are not only homework projects and there is no definite or even recommended time frame for learning through Curiosity Projects. Curiosity Projects have been adapted and implemented as units of study for Elementary, Middle, and High School students. They can also be modified by parents to plan and foster curious learning for their children. The basic template that follows should be viewed as a template or example that can be used to re-design Curiosity Projects for your students, or for children in your particular context.

Timeline Overview

Week 1 - What is Curiosity?
Exploring & Selecting a Topic

Week 2 - What Do Curious People Do to Start Learning?
Planning & Information Gathering

Week 3 - How Do Curious People Gather Information?
Information Gathering Continued

Week 4 - How Do Curious People Gather & Organize Information?
Information Gathering Wrap-up & Beginning to Plan Sharing

Week 5 - How Do Curious People Share Their Learning?
Beginning work on Sharing

Week 6 - How Do Curious People Share Their Learning?
Completing Sharing Preparations & Sharing Event

Project in Brief

1. **Your child will choose** a topic *they* are curious about, or something that *they* want to learn to do.
2. This project will take six weeks.
3. At the end of six weeks, your child will be invited to share their learning with peers. This may also include family members, and other meaningful audiences, on site or virtually.
4. Your focused support and interaction will be required two to three times each week on average. This project is meant to be **flexible** and **enjoyable,** not overwhelming. If it becomes overwhelming, slow down and make accommodations and adjustments to ensure your child is successful and enjoys their Curiosity Project.
5. Your role in this project is to support a learner to succeed. You'll be learning alongside them in "the passenger seat". You might even help them navigate, but they have the steering wheel and they are driving.
6. Your child will require a blank or lined notebook to use as a **Curiosity Journal**. They will use the Curiosity Journal to capture their thinking - the connections, observations, wonderings, questions, plans, and findings throughout the project. A physical Curiosity Journal establishes a concrete place where students can capture, return to, and revise their thinking. Eventually your child will use their journals to reflect on and tell about their learning.

Guidelines for Choosing a Topic

The following guidelines are designed to ensure that students select topics that will enable them to succeed in their learning and experience curiosity as an important drive and starting point for learning.

- The topic must be worth learning about. Learners need to have a "live interest" or compelling curiosity about their topic that will allow them to sustain their learning. Learners should be able to convince others that their chosen topic is worth learning. He or she will be asked to "defend their choice" before moving forward.

- The topic must be a topic *selected by the learner*. Choosing or heavily influencing a student's choice is a shortcut to sabotaging the intended long term impact of Curiosity Projects. Self-direction is the defining characteristic of learning through Curiosity Projects, and a key learning trait that learners will require throughout their lives.
- Learning should have no (or minimal) financial cost.
- Topics/pursuits must be doable or learnable for the learner.

Previous Topics

What follows in the columns is a selection of various topics studied by second and third grade students in the past. Reading through this list may help your child and you to generate many more ideas about what may be possible to learn about.

How Jet engines work

Dangerous Weathers

Dogs

How electricity travels

Horses

How to make bread

Noise-sound

How does paper money work?

Volcanoes

The brain

Cancer

Codes

Air

Jewels and gems

Digestive system

Allergies

Judaism

Cheese

The Philippines

Rockets

Plants

Knights

Worms

Asteroids, meteors, comets

Constellations

Sleep-How does it work? Why do we need sleep?

Teeth

Mosquitoes

How Glass is Made

Oil

How Energy Transfers

The A380 Airbus

Aboriginals of Australia

How Roller Coasters Work

Indian Reptiles

Car Engines

Construction Machines

Echolocation in Animals

Mosquitoes

Singers and Singing as a Profession

Eyes-how they work

Stars

How Earth Started

Guinea Pigs

The Brain

Diamonds

Global Warming

Crystals

Oral Health

Water Conservation

How do birds fly?

How Do Cell Phones Work?

Greek Gods

Vaccinations

Rabbits

Magnetic Levitation Trains

Cloud Computing

Parasites

Jet propulsion

WEEK 1

What is Curiosity?

Monday

Meet with a parent or other adult at home asking these questions:

What is Curiosity? Is it important? Why or Why Not?

Write about what you talked about or thought about in your Curiosity Journal.

Tuesday

Watch at least two of Curious Learner videos linked below:

- Interview with Alex, a game designer http://bit.ly/alexcurious
- Interview with Miss Newcomb, a science teacher http://bit.ly/siencecurious
- Interview with Mr. Sanderson, a web page designer http://bit.ly/curiousweb
- Interview with Ms. Fish, a teacher with a life-long interest in India http://bit.ly/curiousindia

What kinds of things did these curious people **do** to use their curiosity to learn?

What advice did they have for others who might be curious about their topic?

What you are noticing about these curious learners? Capture your thoughts in your Curiosity Journal.

Wednesday

Time to think about what YOU want to learn about. Talk with someone you enjoy thinking with about what YOU are curious about. List these below. Remember, you will be asked to share why you are curious about this topic.

Note: Some children will zero in on a topic immediately. Keep returning to this conversation over the next few days. There is value in considering the possiblities, even if your child is already set on a topic. Having informal conversations around the dinner table, in the car, or on a walk can jumpstart the pleasurable habit of curious learning pursuit in your family.

Friday – Sunday
Time to narrow and choose your Curiosity Project topic. Make sure you choose something you are actively curious about. On Monday, be ready to share what you are curious about and why.

What Do Curious People Do to Start Learning?

Monday - *Capture the story of your curiosity*
Capture your curiosity story. Write the story of how you first became curious about your learning topic. When did your curiosity begin? What caused you to be curious? What does your curiosity feel like? Your answers to these questions will tell yourself and others why this topic is important for you to learn. Capture your answers to these questions in your Curiosity Journal.

Tuesday - *Focusing your topic*
Share your Curiosity Project with someone important to you, even if you have to call them, or write to them. Then, start thinking of the questions you have and the things you want to learn about your topic. Your questions and want-to-learns will power and guide your learning!

Wednesday - *Mapping Questions*
Support children to create a concept map capturing their questions and what they want to learn. Use online mapping software or pencil and paper. Start with a statement "What I want to learn about _____" in the center of the map, and start adding questions starting from that starting point. **This visual document will become the guiding reference document for the rest of the project.** Guide students to glue this document into your Curiosity Journals. Leave blank pages for more questions that will emerge during your project.

Thursday - *Planning Research*
How might I gather information about my topic?

For the next few days you will generate ideas for how you will begin to learn about your topic. Think about these questions:

- Where will I first go to find information on my topic?
- Do I know anyone who might be an expert on my topic?

- Who can help me with my curios learning at home? Who can help me at school?
- How could I use my blog to help get my questions out to more people who might be able to help me?
- How will I take notes when I find answers to my questions or other interesting information?

Capture your ideas and thoughts/ideas/plans in your Curiosity Journal.

Now you're really ready to start learning about your topic. Remember, the concept map with your focus questions should be your guide for the project. Feel free to pencil in new questions as you think of them. Feel free to get started.

WEEK 3

How Do Curious People Gather & Organize Information?

This is the week learners should begin to dive deeply into their topic. They will begin researching and learning referencing the map created in their Curiosity Journals. Your child and you should begin or continue to gather information and learn together. Remember you will have two weeks to gather information. These two weeks will be the time where your friendly guidance, support, and partnership will be most needed. Therefore, there are only two other very quick tasks required during this week.

Monday - *Interview*
Adult: Your job is to interview your child about what they think about this question: **How do curious people gather information?**

Please write down verbatim what the learner says in their Curiosity Journal.

Tuesday - Friday - *Begin gathering information*

Before Monday - *Checking in*
Students, last week you wrote about how you first became interested in this topic and what inspired you to choose your topic. How it is going? Think about the questions below and be ready to talk with your peers about these questions on Monday:

- How is research going?
- What has been most challenging? ...most rewarding or fun?
- Have you learned anything unexpected or unusual?
- Are you more or less interested in your topic now that you are learning more about it?

WEEK 4

How Do Curious People
Gather Information?
(Continued)

Continue gathering information during this week. But you will want to think about how to guide your child through choosing what they want to share what they are learning.

Monday - Friday - *Gathering Information*

Way Leads to Way
Your child may have encountered new information that has them wondering new things. Take some time to assess with your child to see if there are any new questions that should be added to their concept map and pursued. Record any new questions on the concept map with your child and continue pursuing learning.

Finished Gathering Information?
You may begin to work on sharing information during this week.

If your child is done gathering information, they may begin to start working on sharing the project in the next section. Please send me an email if your child is done gathering information.

WEEK 5

How Do Curious People
Share Their Learning?

The main work this week is to help your child consider how to put their presentation together in a way that will help them share with the class or help students learn from their presentations. Therefore, there is only one other very quick task required during this week.

Monday - *Interview conversation:*
> *How do you think you can share your learning?*

Student Sharing Options
Your child may share using other media such as:

- **making a poster** (I can provide posterboard)
- **building a model**
- **making a movie**
- **using other multi-media tools**
- **another way they prefer** (have them check with me first)

IMPORTANT
Sharing should not be an anxiety-producing event. It is also important that students continue to be in charge of their learning as they plan how they will share. *"The student"* must be the obvious answer to the question: "Who is sharing this?" If you or your child are feeling anxious, please let me know so I can help.

Help and support your child to succeed, but don't make it *your* product. Work with your child and think with them, but don't take over or get caught up in how **you** want it to look. If you need to help them cut, or paste, or print etc... that's fine. Just don't take over.

How Do Curious People Share Their Learning?

Sharing - *Teachers, here are two options that we have used in the past. Both worked very well. Our preference is for the first one as it creates more of a sense of an event and celebration atmosphere.*

1. **A Curiosity Gallery** event where all students set up in one space and parents, interested faculty, and other classes attend. This feels more like an event and the visual display of diverse topics inspires learners and visitors to consider new learning possibilities. Providing ways for students to receive written feedback has been successful in the past.

2. **Traditional Presentations.** During these presentations each child is given a time slot to present their learning to a meaningful audience. They present, then field questions and connections from the audience.

An online template is available for use and adaptation - http://bit.ly/curiosityprojects

Curiosity Projects - Resources

In this section you will find letters to parents, a template for interviewing curious learner models in front of your students, a rubric that teachers can use to assess Curiosity Projects, and links to other resources.

Parent Letter Template
Provided to parents prior to the start of Curiosity Projects

Dear Parents,

During the next 6 weeks we will be supporting your child's work during a *Curiosity Project*. The goal of this project is to provide modeling, structure, and practice that support students to learn how to use their curiosity to power their learning. Our aim is to develop learners who initiate and pursue their own learning and develop a disposition to use their curiosity to seek meaningful learning. The project is designed to be done in a relaxed manner over the course of six weeks.

Your role in the project will be to **guide** and **support** a learner in pursuit of what she or he strives to learn. ***You can and should be co-interested and co-curious in their pursuit. But the pursuit is theirs, not yours***. You are supporting a learner to succeed in learning how to learn.

During this project, your child will focus on inquiring into these core questions about curiosity in order to power their learning:
- **What is curiosity?**
- **How do curious learners use their curiosity to initiate their learning?**
- **How do curious learners gather information?**
- **How do curious learners share information?**
- **How do curious learners reflect on their learning?**

You will receive a parent guide in the coming days that will help you support your child's learning. We're looking forward to helping your children learn how to learn using their curiosity!

Sincerely,

xxxxxxxxx

Template for Recruiting and Interviewing Curious Learners

Dear,

Soon my students will embark on a **Curiosity Project** where they explore a topic of interest in a meaningful way. We will begin this unit by studying how passionate, engaged learners pursue their curiosity to learn. We have identified you as someone who uses their curiosity to drive passionate, engaged learning.

Here is my request:

Can I videotape you or interview you in class answering four questions about a passion/interest that you have? During the interview, you will be asked the following questions.

Questions:
1. **How did you first become curious about _____?**
2. **Once you knew you were curious about _____ , how did you gather information about it?**
3. **Once you learned more about _____ , how did/do/have you share(d) what you learned with others?**
4. **What advice would you give someone who was just starting to pursue something they were curious about or interested in?**

Let me know if you are available/interested in helping us out with this project.

Sincerely,

xxxxxxxxx

Check-In Letter Template for Parents

This template is designed to enable teachers to check in with parents. This will help you encourage and support the parents that need it and guard against a negative buzz resulting from parents who are feeling anxious or stuck.

Dear Parents,

I wanted to take a moment to check in with you about how the Curiosity Projects are going at home. Do you need any help or have any questions? Is your child still interested and motivated?

Here are some tips as you and your child go about looking for information to answer their focus questions:

- Keep in mind that this entire project is focused on the process of learning and discovery, not the final product.
- Avoid going on an "Easter-egg hunt" for facts. Approach this with an attitude of investigation, wondering and striving to understand. Facts are even more astounding within this context.
- If, along the way, your child learns something interesting that is unrelated to their topic, have them write this down.
- Remember that primary research is powerful. Can you observe what your child is curious about? Can you email or visit an expert in their topic. Are there online videos of experts talking about what they do in this area?
- Use our school library and librarians. They are more than willing to help both with finding books or online resources.
- Children can get lost in information from books and websites. You are the bridge between your child and the information they are seeking. They will likely need your help to summarize, skim, rephrase, and unpack more complex information.

Reminder: We will have a Research Breakfast tomorrow morning at 8:00am. I will ask you to sit with a child (not your own!) and help them answer some of their focus questions. If you can join us for that morning and have not already told me, let me know! We'd love to have your help.

I hope you are enjoying working on these at home as much as I am enjoying working with your children at school. Keep in touch and let me know how I can help.

Sincerely,

XXXXXXXXX

Curiosity Project Assessment

This is an example of one assessment teachers have used to assess Curiosity Projects. It can be used or adapted to meet assessment needs.

Assessing your learning process, product, and learning reflection
Your final project (product) must include two main components: your information and the sharing of your Curiosity Story, and your reflection on your learning. See the rubric below.

I will interview you and read your Curiosity Journal to learn more about your process.

You will be assessed on:

1. Your Information/Research → *What* you learned.
2. Your Curiosity Journal → *How* you learned it.
3. Your Reflection → *Your thoughts* on the *process* of learning.

After you have chosen how you want to share your information, you will need to decide what you are going to share and how you are going to share it.

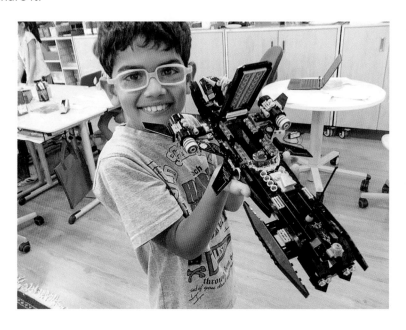

How your *project* will be scored:

	3 Excellent	2 Approaching	1 Needs Improvement
Information	• My information is accurate and clear and you can easily see where I found it (sources). • It is organized and relates to my main topic. • I have obviously worked on this for three weeks and am an enthusiastic expert on my topic and/or process.	• My information is good and usually relates to my main topic. Sources are sometimes included. • It is sometimes hard for others to see how I organized it. • I found some good information, but maybe didn't use all the time I was given.	• My information looks like I'm beginning and sources are not included. • My organization makes it hard for others to follow my thinking. • I could have used my time more effectively and found more/better information
Curiosity Story	• I clearly shared how my idea began, the highs and lows of learning about it, and how I feel about it now.	• I shared a basic story of the beginning, middle and end of my learning process, but with few details.	• My story is hard to follow and is missing details and any reflection.
Reflection in Curiosity Journal*	• My reflection is honest and detailed and shares where I have been and am as a learner.	• My reflection is a start, but is not complete. There is more I could have shared or explained.	• I did not share many of my thoughts and feelings and need to work on this some more.

Gathering Data From Parents

This is a sample parent feedback form http://bit.ly/parentfeed that can be used or adapted to meet feedback needs.

Credits & Sharing

This template was developed over time by educators Beth Hoeppner, Mike Jackson, Sammi Smith, and myself and is undergoing further development by the R&D Department at The American School of Bombay. If you use this template to create your own Curiosity Projects, please feel free to share your work with us at RnD@asbindia.org

Variations

Curiosity Projects require structure. But they are designed to be flexible and adaptable so that educators or parents can create variations that meet their needs and the needs of their learners. In this chapter, you will see examples of how Curiosity Projects have been adapted to create variations for Elementary, Middle, and High School students.

The key elements of a Curiosity Project are:

Curiosity Projects Provide Essential Conditions for Intrinsic Motivation
- Condition of Autonomy
- Condition of Competence
- Condition of Relatedness to Others

Curiosity Projects include the aspects of Holdaway's Natural Learning Model
- Demonstration
- Participation
- Practice
- Performance

Curiosity Projects engage learners in uncovering what curious learners do
- How do curious learners use their curiosity to initiate their learning?
- How do curious learners gather information?
- How do curious learners share information?
- How do curious learners reflect on their learning?

Variation 1

Primetime

Primetime is a variation of the Curiosity Project developed at the Elementary School. Time is set aside each week for students to learn something they were curious about. Using your curiosity to learn doesn't have to be a herculean effort. It can be a matter of setting aside time for students to learn and share their learning. In Grade 5 at the American School of Bombay, Primetime happened once a week in place of traditional homework. At home, students:

- choose what they are curious about or interested in learning.
- record what they chose to learn.
- record simple reflections about their learning.
- record the time they spent learning at home that day.

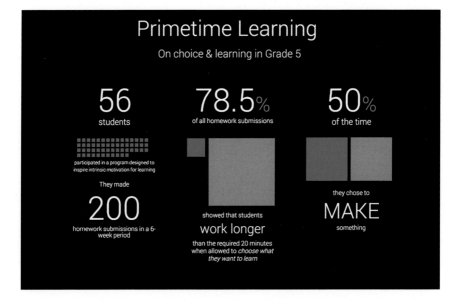

Above is data from 5th grade students who answered a few quick questions everyday after their Primetime Learning.

Easing Your Primetime Path

Here are two templates to ease the path to Primetime:

- A parent letter template that you might choose to make a copy of and customize to fit your class or grade level. http://bit.ly/primeletter
- A Google Form that can be customized for your class or grade level. http://bit.ly/ptimeform

Variation 2

The following is a document shared with seventh and eighth grade students at Hong Kong International School outlining their G8 Self-Motivated Learning (SML) unit that takes place over the course of two months. This course is a variation of a Curiosity Project designed by Middle School Social Studies teachers, Peter Dratz and Jeff Peirce.

G8 SELF-MOTIVATED LEARNING - What would you love to learn?

Introduction: During the next two months, you will be learning about something **you** care about. Instead of having normal teacher directed classes, you are going to direct your own learning. At the end of this project, you will have 5 minutes to present your learning to an audience of your peers and a group of adults. **Your project will be solo.** If you want to include other people in your project (e.g. actors in a short video), that is OK. We will not, however, pull people from other classes to help you with your presentation. If someone from your class is

involved, that work must be done outside of class. Everyone must work on their own SML project during class.

"Self Motivated Learning" - What does it mean? (aka "Genius Hour", The "Curiosity Project", "The Quest", "Google 20%", "Constructivist Learning")

What are you really curious about?

What would you really like to learn . . . to invent . . . to discover?

When I first went to university, I saw a guy standing out in the middle of the quad juggling a soccer ball using both feet and his head equally well. I thought to myself, "I could do that." I walk . . . a lot. Last Spring, on my walks, I identified two dozen types of wild flowers in Hong Kong which I photographed and presented. I called my project "May Flowers". Find something *you* want to learn.

Here's a video that summarizes a project called "Genius Hour": http://bit.ly/genius60

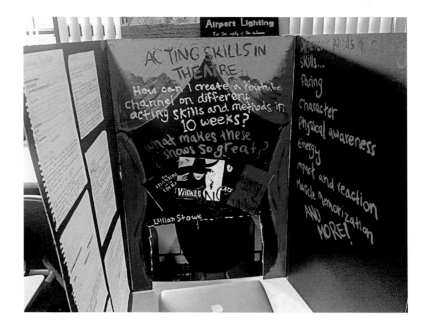

Asking the Question

- There must be a driving question. You must be able to communicate clearly what you want to learn about.
- Your question must involve research and one or more experts/mentors.
- Try to avoid questions that are a part of / extension of something you already do.
- The answer (learning) to your question must be shared.

Knowledge and Understanding: *Questions about Questions*

(Spartan Guide - Asking good questions, Springfield Township HS, http://bit.ly/askmyquestions)

"Which" questions - These questions require that you collect a lot of data and make an informed choice after interpreting the data you have collected.

- Which 20th century woman contributed most towards obtaining rights for women?
- Which type of chocolate is best for your health?
- Which type of energy would be best for Hong Kong?

"How" questions - These questions require that you become aware of all components of the question?

- How can HKIS significantly lower its carbon footprint?
- How can I learn how to play the ukulele?
- How can I learn enough Korean to allow me to begin interacting with my friends in Korean?

"Should" questions - These questions require you to take a position or a stand on an issue based on available information?

- Should we clone human beings?
- Should Hong Kong be allowed to select who runs for Chief Executive?
- Should we forbid students' access to technology during PEAK trips?

"Why" questions - Understanding and explaining relationships to get a clear understanding of complicated issues?

- Why do kids like junk food?
- Why do people believe in God?
- Why did the Chinese simplify characters after liberation in 1949?

"Possibility" questions - Exploring actual research and investigation to create an hypothesis

- Is time travel possible?
- Is there a way to physically travel into deep space?
- What is the importance of prime numbers?

Research and Investigation: How can you most effectively learn what you would love to learn?

You must do significant research. Research can either be conventional searching for information on-line or hard copy, but it can also be hands-on, trial and error research. You need to keep a record of your research. This could be in the form of hand written notes, an electronic journal, a video record, photographs, or a combination of the above. You will also need to find an expert/mentor who you can communicate with (in person or electronically). You will use your findings in creating your presentation.

Presentation and Communication: What would be an effective way of demonstrating what I have learned? What do I present if I fail to accomplish what I set out to achieve? How could "failure" demonstrate "success" in learning. You will have 5-10 minutes to demonstrate your learning to the audience.

Day 1 - Deciding on the Question
Balancing Desirability, Viability, Sustainability, and Feasibility
- **Desirability** - What do I want to do?
  - This is wide open (How does FB work? How do you sing Peking opera? How do you make an electric car? How do you play the ukulele? How do you dance the tango?)
- **Viability** - *What can I do?* "Viable" means "able to live"; you need to pick something you are comfortable sharing both with your classmates and their parents (they will be invited); maybe when you begin looking at Peking opera, you realize you need to learn to sing falsetto; maybe you there's no one in this class you would be comfortable dancing the tango with.
- **Sustainability** - *Do I really want to spend 9 hours doing this?* Are you willing to commit the next nine class periods to doing serious research and practice learning about your topic?
- **Feasibility** - *What is practical?* Do you have time to accomplish your plan? Could you make an electric car in class? (You can work outside of class, of course, but you must have SML work which you can do in class during each session. Do you have the available resources to pursue your topic?

Hope, Confidence, and Insight - Caution: This is NOT an easy project!
You are going to start off with something you really like. It fits all of the above criteria. You may however get frustrated and you will hit some

low points. Try to work through those points and you will continue to make progress - but not always as fast as you would like to.

Daily Check-ins - after each session of research, we want to know three things from our students:

1) What did they learn in their research today?
2) What is their plan for their next session?
3) What is their plan for sharing their learning? You will use the following Google Spreadsheet to report in at the end of each class.

A Pep Talk from Kid President to You - http://bit.ly/kidppep

20% - http://bit.ly/20timelearn

Variation 3

How Curiosity Found a Home in the Art Studio
By Suzie Boss
Originally published in *Future Forwards* Volume 2

"Inquiry is the personal path of questioning, investigating, and reasoning that takes us from not knowing to knowing."
– from Thinking Through Project-Based Learning

Good questions are at the heart of the inquiry experience. When investigations are guided by questions that students care about answering, engagement increases. The same goes for teacher learning. Teachers who are willing to ask hard questions about their own practice model what it means to be a continuous, curious learner.

Take the case of Karen Fish, visual art teacher in the High School at the American School of Bombay. Earlier this year, the veteran educator found herself wondering about strategies that might deepen student engagement. She was motivated in part by the emphasis on student ownership in the ISTE National Educational Technology Standards for Students. She also was curious how she might make better use of the time at the end of units, when some students finish assignments sooner than others. It's not always the same students who are left "in the gap," as she puts it. "Some are more comfortable with drawing. Others just take off when it's a sculptural project. They work at different speeds on different assignments, and it's unpredictable."

Fish has tried filling the gap by encouraging students to pursue individual interests. "They would start off so excited, but then I could see the motivation going away as soon as we moved on to a new unit [that the teacher assigned]. They had no time to continue working on something they cared about. I wasn't honoring their interests by giving them what they really needed, which was time," she says.

Fish was intrigued, too, by the Curiosity Project, an immersion in student-directed in the elementary school at ASB. The idea was pioneered by Scot Hoffman, now on ASB's R&D team, when he was an elementary teacher. Curiosity Projects involves students exploring topics they are curious about as they participate in an extended homework project. Read more about the Curiosity Project in this Edutopia post (http://bit.ly/curioushomework).

And so Fish posed this question: What if she modified the Curiosity Project as an in-class assignment for her art students? What might they produce if given the freedom—and time—to explore a visual art style that makes them curious? In the following interview, she reflects on what happened next.

Why did you make this an in-class project, rather than assign as homework?

Karen Fish: If I'm really going to honor students' motivation and interests, I realized I need to give them time. So I handed over 12 class period for this project. That meant shortening some other units and picking up the pace. I thought that would be a good thing. We get too bogged down sometimes. This would be a nice, short unit with a lot of student ownership.

Did students quickly identify what they wanted to work on? How did you help those who struggled to come up with a project idea?

KF: Some did struggle at first. If they seemed a bit lost, I asked them, what do you really care about? One boy wears a baseball cap to school every day. Baseball is clearly his passion. When I pointed that out to him, his eyes got all shiny and he came alive. Another boy, new to the school, said he had only worked in black and white. It turns out he loves the ocean—he's a surfer. So here was a chance for him to use color to explore drawing waves. Other students brought in a specific image or example from an artist who inspires them. The inspiration was different for each student.

How did you structure the project?

KF: I knew I was going to have a lot of kids doing different things. How was I going to give feedback to everybody? We set up a Google Doc and

I had them reflect after every class. Then I could respond with resources or individualized instruction. I might share a YouTube video or book with one or show another something about a technique like dry brush.

What was challenging about this for you, as a teacher?

KF: At first, I wasn't sure how much I should get involved. This was supposed to be student-directed learning, right? I wanted to let them find their own way and not keep telling them, here's how you do this. But at first I pulled back too much. I was missing the teachable moments. So I talked with Scot (Hoffman), and he reassured me that it's OK to help them in a project like this. Then I started guiding them more.

What did you notice about students' reflections?

KF: One girl started with a ceramics project. She made candleholders, kind of sculptural, but not very challenging. She told me, 'I can make clay fast. I want to try something harder.' So then she tried painting sunflowers, inspired by Monet. There are layers of paint behind the surface of her canvas—a lot of starting, stopping, starting over. She has a lovely sense of textures. She has discovered a clear talent toward painting and she wants to explore this more. She has found a confidence that a lot of kids don't have.

Another girl, new to the school, arrived with very little English. I don't speak Japanese. So we've had to do a lot of gesturing. She showed me a photo of a dock jutting into the ocean, showing a vanishing point. That inspired her. She had to learn techniques to get the sky and clouds just the way she wanted. I was able to provide just-in-time instruction so she could go forward. She's so visually aware—she'll just take my hand and point, show me something she wants to learn to do. And now her English is coming right along, too. She has such a positive attitude toward learning.

How did you assess this project?

KF: Well, I have to grade! I can't give up 12 class periods just for fun. It occurred to me early on that some students had aimed really high. They might not have polished studio projects ready by the end, but they've taken a risk to try something big. I don't want to penalize them for risk taking. Normally, I grade a project 60 percent on the final product and 40 percent on their reflection and investigation—the process. I was honest with the class and told them I had this dilemma about how to grade.

I explained that some students are just flying on the reflection and process part, but the studio work is not coming out how they want yet. Others have fabulous products, but don't like to reflect on their process. I suggested flipping the usual formula, and putting more emphasis on process and reflection. Well, when I said that, some students said, 'Yay!' and others said 'Oh, no.' So I asked them why, and then told them I'd need to go away and think about it.

The solution I came up with is a sliding scale. I've shared the rubric for grading, and it's up to each student to slide the percentages around. How much shall we emphasize your product in grading? How much your process? Each student sets the parameters. That has become something else for them to think about, and I think it's making assessment more valuable. The goal is for everyone to be successful, and to think about what they've set out to accomplish.

What have you noticed about motivation in this project?

KF: Many students have worked harder than they have on any art project before. Some are taking work home and continuing to work on it there. One girl started with an idea of a large digital portrait that she would manipulate with type. She began with one family member, but as she's learning more about technique, she's going on to produce portraits of her entire family. And each one's getting better.

What will you take away from this project into future art assignments?

KF: Everyone's curious about something, aren't they? I've seen such a diversity of projects. I admit, that's been a little scary for me as a teacher. I've had students attempting techniques I know nothing about, especially when it comes to digital tools. But then I get to say, how did you do that? Can you teach me? I think that's a good thing for us all.

What did art students think about the Curiosity Project? Here are a few reflections that they shared while the project was still underway.

John: I'm originally from Santa Barbara, Calif. My whole family surfs. This is my first real art class. I like that I've had the chance to decide what I want to make and how to use my time. I like setting my own goals and reflecting on my own progress. Right now I'm working on a picture of a surfer in the barrel, about to  head into a wave. I'm blending pastels to get the colors just the way I want them, the blues and greens. I know just what they should look like. I've been there myself so many times.

 **Eunji:** I'm painting sunflowers in the style of Monet. He's my favorite artist. I'm happy with how the flowers look but I'm struggling with the pot, getting the color and light right. It's only my second time using acrylics. There are probably three versions on the canvas behind what you see! My mom has a place waiting for this painting on our living room wall.

Meenu: This is a combination of 2D and 3D. I'm drawing on the Japanese style of making everyday objects seem more dramatic. This project has involved a lot of time management. It's all about you and the goals you set for yourself. When I add the sculpture—the 3D—it will be like a person looking out from a balcony.

Eunji: I'm making a big portrait of my brother's face. He's 10. It's a new style for me. It looks like scribbling, but I like how it adds texture to the portrait. I kind of panicked when we started this project. I'm not used to coming up with my own ideas. It can be hard to direct myself, to know what to do next. But I'm enjoying the final product. It think it captures how active my brother is. That's a big part of his personality.

Assessing Curious Learners

Curiosity Projects are courses of learning designed to intrinsically motivate, grow students' awareness of how they can use their curiosity to initiate, plan, and regulate their own learning. The projects are designed to inspire learning, make grit worth having, and draws them into passionate, engaged learning and living. How do you assess these in learners?

In *Ungifted: Intelligence Redefined, the Truth about Talent, Practice, Creativity, and the Many Paths to Greatness*, cognitive psychologist and former special education student, Kauffman shares research on the conditions for intrinsic motivation, inspiration, self-regulation, passion, and hope. Each of these has some type of research validated scale or instrument. These scales and instruments can guide us towards assessing and developing the kinds of learners we need to see thriving in our schools, our classrooms, and our families. Taking these scales and adapting them so that they can be used in the everyday practical environment of schools and homes has tremendous potential to transform teaching and learner development.

References

Adkins, A. (January 2015). *Majority of U.S. Employees Not Engaged Despite Gains in 2014.* Retrieved from http://www.gallup.com/poll/181289/majority-employees-not-engaged-despite-gains-2014.aspx

Anderson, C. (n.d.). *The Longtail, in a Nutshell.* Retrieved August 11, 2015, from http://www.longtail.com/about.html

Engel, S. (2013, February 1). *The Case for Curiosity. Educational Leadership*, 36-40.

Fernández-Aráoz, C. (2014). 21st Century talent spotting. *Harvard business review, 92*(6), 46-54.

Gallup Inc. (2014). *Gallup Student Poll 2014 Overall US Report.* Retrieved from http://www.gallup.com/services/180029/gallup-student-poll-2014-overall-report.aspx

Gruber, M. J., Gelman, B. D., & Ranganath, C. (2014). States of curiosity modulate hippocampus-dependent learning via the dopaminergic circuit.*Neuron, 84*(2), 486-496.

Heath, Chip, and Dan Heath. (2007) *Made to stick: Why some ideas survive and others die*. [Kindle Version] Retrieved from Amazon.com 1391

Hoffman, S. (2014). *Curiosity Projects: Autonomy-Supportive Home Learning in Second Grade.* (Unpublished thesis). Boston University, Boston Massachusetts.

Kang, M. J., Hsu, M., Krajbich, I. M., Loewenstein, G., McClure, S. M., Wang, J. T. Y., & Camerer, C. F. (2009). *The wick in the candle of learning epistemic curiosity activates reward circuitry and enhances memory. Psychological Science, 20*(8), 963-973.

Piotrowski, J. T., Litman, J. A., & Valkenburg, P. (2014). Measuring epistemic curiosity in young children. *Infant and Child Development*, *23*(5), 542-553.

Thrash, T. M., & Elliot, A. J. (2004). Inspiration: core characteristics, component processes, antecedents, and function. *Journal of personality and social psychology*, *87*(6), 957.

Torrance, E. P. (1983). The importance of falling in love with" something." *Creative Child & Adult Quarterly*.

Weaver, C. (2002). Teaching Reading and Developing Literacy: Contrasting Perspectives. *In Reading process and practice: From socio-psycholinguistics to whole language* (Third Edition ed., p. 15). Portsmouth, NH: Heinemann Educational Books.

About the Author

 International educator, Scot Hoffman is a big believer in the power of curiosity to drive learning. After nearly two decades of teaching around the globe, he also realizes that school isn't always so hospitable to inquiring minds. (As Einstein said, "It's a miracle that curiosity survives formal education.") That's why Hoffman has developed The Curiosity Project as a self-directed learning experience that engages students, parents, and teachers as collaborators in inquiry. You can connect with Scot via Twitter @bombayscot and email: hoffmans@asbindia.org